FARMYARD STORIES

The Cow

Kingfisher Books, Grisewood & Dempsey Ltd,
Elsley House, 24–30 Great Titchfield Street,
London W1P 7AD

This reformatted edition first published in 1992
by Kingfisher Books
2 4 6 8 10 9 7 5 3 1

Originally published in 1989 in paperback as
Farm Animal Stories: The Cow by Kingfisher Books

Copyright © Grisewood & Dempsey Ltd 1989, 1992

BRITISH LIBRARY CATALOGUING IN PUBLICATION DATA
A catalogue record for this book is available from the British Library

ISBN 0 86272 984 X

Series adviser: Dr Bryan Howard, University of Sheffield
Edited by Jacqui Bailey and Veronica Pennycook
Cover design by Cooper/Wilson
Cover illustration by Steve Holden/*John Martin & Artists Ltd*
Phototypeset by Southern Positives and Negatives
(SPAN), Lingfield, Surrey
Printed in Portugal

FARMYARD STORIES

The Cow

By Angela Royston
Illustrated by Bob Bampton

Kingfisher Books

The young cows have spent all winter in the barn but now it is spring and the farmer brings them out into the fields. They smell the fresh grass and pull up huge mouthfuls of it. They run across the field in the bright sunshine, happy to be outside again.

The black cow sees that the gate to the next field has been left open. She pushes through it and the other cows follow her. This field is full of long grass and clover. The cows love the damp sweet smells and they eat all they can.

The farmer knows that clover will make the cows ill so he drives them back to their own field. But later that day the black cow's aching stomach swells up with gas. She is so uncomfortable she cannot lie down.

The other cows are ill too, so that evening the vet comes. She decides to make a small hole in the black cow's belly to let the gas out but the other cows just need medicine. Next day they are all well again.

Summer comes, and the cows are nearly two years old. They are grazing alongside the riverbank. The black cow pulls the grass into her mouth with her long tongue. Flies buzz round her and she flicks her tail to try and drive them away.

The leader of the herd moves away from the riverside and the others follow her. They stand in the shade of a big tree and chew their cud. They bring some of the grass back into their mouths, chew it slowly, and then swallow it again.

The next day the farmer puts a bull into the field. The black cow is curious and wanders over to have a better look at him. They sniff each other and stay close together all day. The bull paws the ground and nuzzles her side. He knows by her smell that she is ready to mate.

The days pass and winter comes. The nights are very cold and there is less grass to eat in the field. One rainy afternoon as the cows huddle together by the hedge the farmer comes to take them back to the barn.

The floor is covered with straw and there is plenty of hay to eat. The black cow tosses the straw with her head and kicks it up with her heels. She hears the farm dog barking and a tractor rumbling by.

The black cow stays in the barn all winter. During the day the hens peck in the straw for grain, and at night the mice sometimes come looking for grain too. A new calf is growing inside the cow and as winter turns to spring her belly grows larger. Ten months after mating, her calf is ready to be born.

The farmer puts her in a quiet pen with lots of straw. She lies down and a few hours later her calf is born. She licks him all over.

The black cow nuzzles her newborn calf and helps him to stand on his wobbly legs. At first the calf falls down again but soon he is strong enough to reach her udders and suck milk from her teats.

The cow can feel the little calf trembling
against her side. She moos softly to him and
they lie down together. The little calf is warm
and tired and soon falls asleep.

17

When the calf is a few days old he is moved into a pen with other calves. He misses his mother but now he is old enough to suck milk from a teat attached to a bucket. The farmer takes his mother to be milked.

She stands in a stall and four rubber cups are placed over her teats. She munches feed from a trough and listens to the hum of machinery as the milk is gently pumped from her udders.

It is summertime again. The cow has not seen her calf since he was very young and now she has forgotten about him. It is late afternoon and her udders are full of milk. She waits by the gate because she knows it will soon be milking time.

When the farmer comes she slowly follows the other cows up the lane to the milking parlour. A new calf is growing inside her. It will be born next spring.

Good ✓

More About Cows

There are many different types of dairy cow. The cow in this story is a Holstein cow. Holsteins and Friesians give the most milk of all dairy cows.

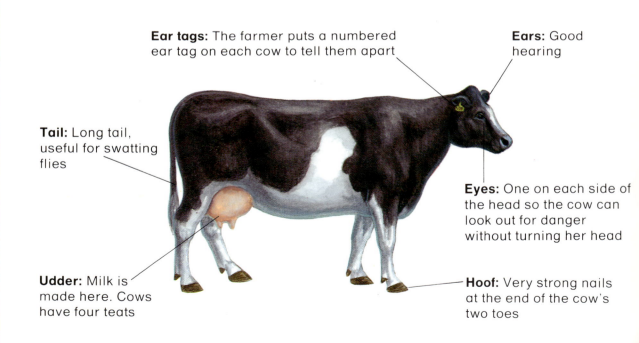

Ear tags: The farmer puts a numbered ear tag on each cow to tell them apart

Ears: Good hearing

Tail: Long tail, useful for swatting flies

Eyes: One on each side of the head so the cow can look out for danger without turning her head

Udder: Milk is made here. Cows have four teats

Hoof: Very strong nails at the end of the cow's two toes

The Brown Swiss is a very old breed of cow. They used to pull ploughs and other farm machinery. Now they are popular in the high mountains of Switzerland. Jersey and Guernsey cows give very creamy milk. Milk can be used to make butter, yoghurt and many kinds of cheese.

Brown Swiss

Friesian

Jersey

Guernsey

A cow has four stomachs. The first two store the food as she grazes. Later she brings balls or cuds of grass back into her mouth and chews them until they are mushy. She swallows them again and they then pass to the other stomachs to be digested.

Some Special Words

Bull A male cow.

Calf A young cow. Cows usually have only one calf at a time.

Clover A small three-leaved plant which often grows among grass. Too much young clover is poisonous to cows.

Cow Female cows give milk for a year after their calf is born so they are mated every year.

Heifer A young cow before it has had calves and can be milked.

Herd A group of cows. One cow leads the herd. A herd of cows tends to keep together. The leader decides when they will all graze, chew their cud and rest. She is usually the first to go into the milking shed.

Vet A person trained to look after sick animals.